KU-523-820

FRESH FROM THE OVEN

PIES & TARTS

HARBOUR
BOOKS

CONTENTS

ASPARAGUS FLAN

SERVES 4-6

SHORTCRUST PASTRY:

2 cups (8 oz, 250 g) all-purpose (plain) flour
pinch of salt, optional
2 oz (60 g) chilled butter or firm margarine
2 oz (60 g) shortening (lard)
approx. 4 tablespoons cold water, to mix

FILLING:

1 tablespoon butter
1 onion, finely chopped or grated
2 eggs, lightly beaten
$^1/_2$ cup (4 fl oz, 125 ml) light (single) cream
4 oz (125 g) tasty cheese, grated
$^1/_2$ teaspoon French mustard
salt and black pepper
12 canned or cooked asparagus spears, drained

Shortcrust pastry: Sift flour and salt into cold mixing bowl. Cut in butter and shortening with a palette knife, coating with flour. Rub fat into flour with cool fingertips, lifting up and rubbing from a height to lighten and aerate. When mixture resembles breadcrumbs, shake bowl gently and any lumps will rise to surface. Squeeze and if dry, fat is rubbed in sufficiently, but if they feel greasy, continue rubbing in.

Sprinkle cold water over gradually and mix in with a palette knife until mixture begins to form lumps which leave side of bowl cleanly. Knead dough together lightly with a clean, cool hand. You can use an electric mixer or a food processor.

Roll out and use to line an 8 inch (20 cm) flan pan (tin).

Preheat oven to 400°F (200°C, Gas Mark 6).

Sauté onion in butter until soft. Beat eggs and cream together, stir in cheese, mustard, salt, and pepper, then cooled onion. Pour into pastry case, and arrange asparagus spears on top.

Bake in oven for 10 minutes, reduce oven temperature to 375°F (190°C, Gas Mark 5) and bake for 30 minutes longer or until set. Serve warm or cold.

CARROT FLAN

WHOLEWHEAT (WHOLEMEAL) PASTRY:

1 ³/₄ cups (8 oz, 250 g) wholewheat (wholemeal) flour, medium or coarse ground

1 teaspoon salt

4 oz (125 g) butter or firm margarine

cold water, to mix

FILLING:

1 lb (500 g) young carrots, cooked and mashed

2 egg yolks

¹/₃ cup (2 ¹/₂ fl oz, 75 ml) reduced cream

4 tablespoons grated tasty cheese

3 tablespoons finely chopped chives (or onion greens)

¹/₂ teaspoon finely chopped fresh rosemary

salt and pepper

Wholewheat shortcrust pastry: Sift flour and salt into cold mixing bowl. Cut in butter and shortening with a palette knife, coating with flour. Rub fat into flour with cool fingertips, lifting up and rubbing from a height to lighten and aerate.

When mixture resembles breadcrumbs, shake bowl gently and any lumps will rise to surface. Squeeze and if dry, fat is rubbed in sufficiently, but if they feel greasy, continue rubbing in.

Sprinkle cold water over gradually and mix in with a palette knife until mixture begins to form lumps which leave side of bowl cleanly. Knead dough together lightly with a clean, cool hand.

You can use an electric mixer or a food processor.

Roll out and use to line an 8 inch (20 cm) flan pan (tin). Bake "blind" in preheated oven (300°F, 150°C, Gas Mark 3) for 20 minutes. Leave oven on (350°F, 180°C, Gas Mark 4).

Beat into carrots, the egg yolks, cream, cheese, chives, rosemary, salt, and pepper. Spoon mixture into pastry case. Bake for about 30 minutes or until filling is firm. Serve warm, with green salad.

CHICKEN & PARSLEY PIE

SERVES 6

PUFF PASTRY:

8 oz (250 g) unsalted butter
2 cups (8 oz, 250 g) all-purpose (plain) flour
pinch of salt, optional
1 teaspoon lemon juice
cold water, to mix

FILLING:

6 chicken breasts, skinned and trimmed
salt and peppercorns
sprig of thyme
sprig of parsley
1 oz (30 g) butter
6 French shallots, or scallions (spring onions), finely chopped
4 oz (125 g) button mushrooms (champignons), sliced
1 cup finely chopped parsley
salt and pepper
2 tablespoons wholewheat (wholemeal) flour
3 hard-cooked (boiled) eggs, sliced
egg white, for glazing

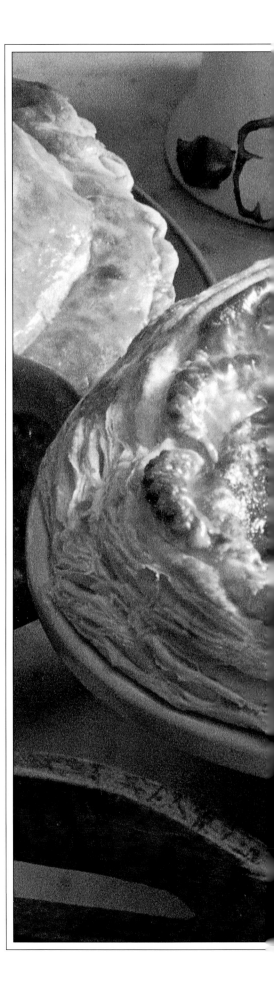

Place chicken in a saucepan with a little salt, a few peppercorns, and sprigs of thyme and parsley; add water to cover. Cover saucepan and cook gently for about 30 minutes. Preheat oven to 400°F (200°C, Gas Mark 6).

Strain off and reserve stock. Dice meat. Heat butter in frying pan, add shallots, mushrooms, parsley, salt, and pepper, and sauté for 5 minutes. Stir in flour and cook for a few minutes. Pour in $^1/_2$ cup (4 fl oz, 125 ml) chicken stock and continue whisking until the mixture thickens. Mix in meat and adjust seasonings. Place half of mixture in base of a deep, ovenproof dish. Arrange sliced eggs on top, then cover with remainder of the chicken mixture.

Puff pastry: Make and chill pastry according to instructions for *Economical Steak and Kidney Pie* (page 12).

Roll out the pastry and cover pie dish. Crimp around edges, cut three or four vents in the top. Decorate top with remnants of pastry. Brush lightly with a little beaten egg white. Bake in oven for 15 minutes, then reduce oven temperature to 325°F (160°C, Gas Mark 3) and continue baking for about 30 minutes. Serve hot.

EASY VEGETABLE PIZZA

SERVES 4-5

2 cups (8 oz, 250 g) self-rising (raising) flour
$^1/_4$ cup (2 oz, 60 g) butter or margarine
salt and pepper
1 teaspoon dried oregano
1 egg, beaten
3 tablespoons milk or skimmed milk
1–2 cloves garlic, crushed
1 large onion, peeled and chopped
1 tablespoon vegetable oil
1 lb (500 g) tomatoes, peeled and sliced or a 14 oz (440 g) canned peeled tomatoes,
partly drained and sliced
2 tablespoons tomato paste (purée)
$^1/_2$ teaspoon Worcestershire sauce
4 oz (125 g) button mushrooms (champignons), sliced
1 can anchovy filets, drained (optional)
10–12 black olives, halved and pitted (stoned)
2 oz (60 g) cheddar or mozarella cheese

Sift flour into a bowl and rub in butter finely. Add a pinch of salt, pepper, and oregano; add egg and sufficient milk to mix to a fairly soft but manageable dough. Pat out dough on a floured surface to a round approx. $^3/_4$ inch (2 cm) thick and 8–9 inches (20–23 cm) diameter. Put on a well-floured or greased baking tray.

Fry garlic and onion in oil until soft. Add tomatoes, tomato paste, Worcestershire sauce, seasonings and cook for about 5 minutes until soft. Add mushrooms and continue for 1 to 2 minutes.

Spread tomato mixture over dough and arrange a lattice of anchovy filets over it. Dot with pieces of olive and either sprinkle with grated cheddar or arrange slices of mozzarella over all.

Cook in fairly hot oven (400°F, 200°C, Gas Mark 6) for 30 to 40 minutes until firm and cheese is brown. Serve hot or cold.

ECONOMICAL STEAK & KIDNEY PIE

2 lb (1 kg) stewing beef
4 oz (125 g) ox kidney, or 2 sheep kidneys
1 tablespoon all-purpose (plain) flour
salt and pepper
2 tablespoons oil
1 medium onion, chopped
$^1/_2$ cup (4 fl oz, 125 ml) stock
2 teaspoons all-purpose (plain) flour
2 teaspoons butter

PUFF PASTRY:

8 oz (250 g) unsalted butter, flattened to $^1/_2$ inch (5mm) square and cooled
2 cups (8 oz, 250 g) all-purpose (plain) flour
pinch of salt, optional
1 teaspoon lemon juice
cold water, to mix
beaten egg, for glazing

Cut meat into small cubes. Clean and trim and dice kidney. Toss meat and kidney in flour mixed with salt and pepper. Heat oil and sauté onion until golden. Add meat and kidney, cook until browned. Transfer onions and meat to a small saucepan, add stock, cover saucepan and simmer gently for 1$^1/_2$ hours or until meat is tender.

Blend 2 teaspoons of flour and 2 teaspoons of butter, and drop into simmering liquid in tiny pieces, stirring until it thickens. Spoon meat and liquid into a pie dish. Preheat oven to 475°F (240°C, Gas Mark 9).

Puff pastry: Sieve flour, and salt into large mixing bowl. With a palette knife mix in lemon juice and sufficient cold water to form an elastic dough. You can use an electric mixer or a food processor. Turn dough onto a floured flat surface and knead until smooth and elastic but not sticky.

On a lightly-floured surface roll dough out to a rectangle twice as big as the butter pat. Place butter on top half of dough, fold the bottom half over. Roll out in a long strip, taking care that butter does not break through. Fold strip of pastry in three — folding the bottom third up and the top third down. Cool in refrigerator for 10 to 15 minutes, roll and fold into three twice, placing folded edge alternately to the left. Repeat rolling and folding processes until pastry has had seven rolls and folds. Wrap dough in waxed (greaseproof) paper and chill well before use.

Roll out pastry and cover pie dish. Trim edges, cut several steam vents in top and decorate with pastry scraps. Brush with beaten egg.

Bake in oven for 20 minutes, then reduce temperature to 350°F (180°C, Gas Mark 4) and bake for 40 minutes longer or until crust is crisp and golden.

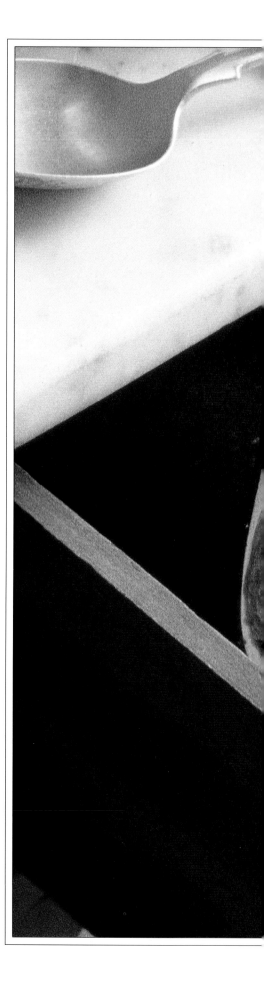

HEARTY WHOLEWHEAT (WHOLEMEAL) VEGETARIAN PIE

SERVES 6–8

WHOLEWHEAT SHORTCRUST PASTRY FOR DOUBLE CRUST PIE:

1 ³/₄ cups (8 oz, 250 g) wholewheat (wholemeal) flour, medium or coarse ground

1 teaspoon salt

4 oz (125 g) butter or firm margarine

cold water, to mix

FIRST LAYER:

¹/₂ cup (4 oz, 125 g) cooked brown rice

4 scallions (spring onions) or French shallots, chopped

2 tablespoons plain yogurt

2 tablespoons grated parmesan cheese

2 tablespoons chopped parsley

freshly ground pepper

SECOND LAYER:

8 oz (250 g) ricotta cheese

1 cup cooked and chopped English spinach or Swiss chard (beet)

3 tablespoons grated parmesan cheese

salt and pepper

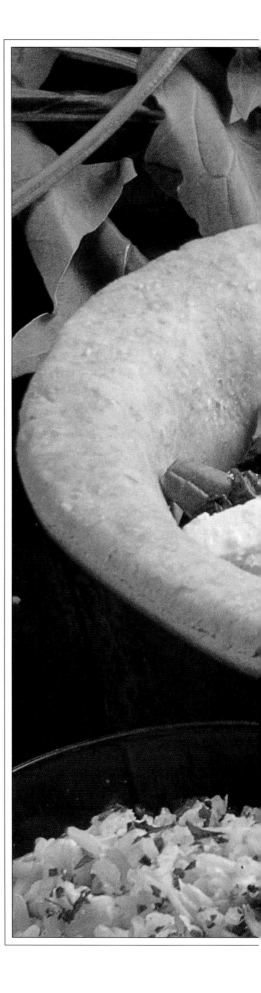

Preheat oven to 350°F (180°C, Gas Mark 4).

Wholewheat shortcrust pastry: Sift flour and salt into cold mixing bowl. Cut in butter and shortening with a palette knife, coating with flour. Rub fat into flour with cool fingertips, lifting up and rubbing from a height to lighten and aerate.

When mixture resembles breadcrumbs, shake bowl gently and any lumps will rise to surface. Squeeze and if dry, fat is rubbed in sufficiently, but if they feel greasy, continue rubbing in.

Sprinkle cold water over gradually and mix in with a palette knife until mixture begins to form lumps which leave side of bowl cleanly. Knead dough together lightly with a clean, cool hand.

You can use an electric mixer or a food processor.

Roll out two-thirds of pastry and line a 9 x 8 inch (23 x 20 cm) pie dish.

First layer: Mix together all ingredients and spoon into pastry.

Second layer: Cream ricotta cheese. Stir in spinach, parmesan cheese, salt, and pepper. Spread over rice. Add grated cheddar cheese for extra flavor if desired.

Roll out remainder of pastry and place it on top of filling. Pinch pastry edges together and cut a few vents in top. Brush surface with a little milk and add a sprinkle of parmesan cheese if desired.

Bake for about 50 minutes. Take out of oven and cut into squares.

HERBED VEGETABLE FLAN

SERVES 4–6

WHOLEWHEAT (WHOLEMEAL) SHORTCRUST PASTRY:

1 3/4 cups (8 oz, 250 g) wholewheat (wholemeal) flour, medium or coarse ground

1 teaspoon salt

4 oz (125 g) butter or firm margarine

cold water, to mix

FILLING:

1 tablespoon butter

2 tablespoons wholewheat (wholemeal) flour

15 fl oz (475 ml) canned vegetable juice

2 small zucchini (courgettes) thinly sliced

2 small carrots, grated

1 small onion, thinly sliced

1 clove garlic, crushed

1 teaspoon chopped fresh herbs

2 oz (60 oz) mushrooms, sliced

TOPPING:

1 1/2 oz (45 g) butter

1 clove garlic, crushed

1 cup (2 oz, 60 g) fresh wholewheat (wholemeal) breadcrumbs

1/2 cup (2 oz, 60 g) grated tasty cheese

2 tablespoons chopped parsley

Wholewheat shortcrust pastry: Sift flour and salt into cold mixing bowl. Cut in butter and shortening with a palette knife, coating with flour. Rub fat into flour with cool fingertips, lifting up and rubbing from a height to lighten and aerate.

When mixture resembles breadcrumbs, squeeze and if dry, fat is rubbed in sufficiently, but if they feel greasy, continue rubbing in. Sprinkle cold water over gradually and mix in with a palette knife until mixture begins to form lumps which leave side of bowl cleanly. Knead dough together lightly with a clean, cool hand.

Roll out pastry thinly and with it line a 10 inch (25 cm) flan pan (tin). Bake "blind" in preheated oven at 350°F (180°C, Gas Mark 4) until golden.

Filling: Melt butter in saucepan. Add flour and cook for several minutes, stirring constantly. Gradually stir in vegetable juice and whisk until smooth. Add zucchini, carrots, onion, garlic, and herbs. Simmer over low heat until just tender and mixture thickens. Add mushrooms and cook for another minute or two, cool.

Preheat oven to 375°F (190°C, Gas Mark 5). Spoon filling into pastry case.

Topping: Melt butter, add crushed garlic, and sauté for a minute or two. Add breadcrumbs and stir until crumbs are coated with butter. Take off heat; stir in cheese and parsley. Spread onto vegetable filling. Bake for 10 to 15 minutes or until topping is crisp and brown. Serve hot or warm.

NEAPOLITAN QUICHE

SERVES 4–6

WHOLEWHEAT (WHOLEMEAL) PASTRY:

1 ³/4 cups (8 oz, 250 g) wholewheat (wholemeal) flour, medium or coarse ground

1 teaspoon salt

4 oz (125 g) butter or firm margarine

cold water, to mix

FILLING:

2 tablespoons butter

1 white onion, chopped

¹/2 clove garlic, crushed

2 tablespoons finely chopped red or green bell pepper (capsicum)

3 tomatoes, sliced

1 teaspoon fresh basil or ¹/2 teaspoon dried basil

salt and pepper

3 oz (90 g) tasty cheese, grated

3 eggs

1 cup (8 fl oz, 250 ml) milk

2 slices green bell pepper (capsicum)

3 small tomatoes, quartered

8 black olives, pitted (stoned) and slivered

Wholewheat pastry: Sift flour and salt into cold mixing bowl. Cut in butter and shortening with a palette knife, coating with flour. Rub fat into flour with cool fingertips, lifting up and rubbing from a height to lighten and aerate. When mixture resembles breadcrumbs, shake bowl gently and any lumps will rise to surface. Squeeze and if dry, fat is rubbed in sufficiently, but if they feel greasy, continue rubbing in.

Sprinkle cold water over gradually and mix in with a palette knife until mixture begins to form lumps which leave side of bowl cleanly. Knead dough together lightly with a clean, cool hand.

You can use an electric mixer or a food processor.

Preheat oven to 375°F (190°C, Gas Mark 5). Line a 9 inch (23 cm) flan dish with pastry.

Heat 1 tablespoon of butter and sauté onion, garlic, and chopped pepper until tender. Remove from pan.

Add second tablespoon of butter to pan, and add tomato slices; fry gently until just tender, drain and arrange on pastry case. Sprinkle with basil, salt, and pepper. Spoon sautéed onion-garlic-peppers into flan. Add grated cheese. Beat eggs lightly and add milk; pour carefully into flan. Arrange bell pepper slices, tomatoes, and olives on top.

Bake for 35 to 40 minutes or until the filling is set and golden brown. May be eaten hot or cold.

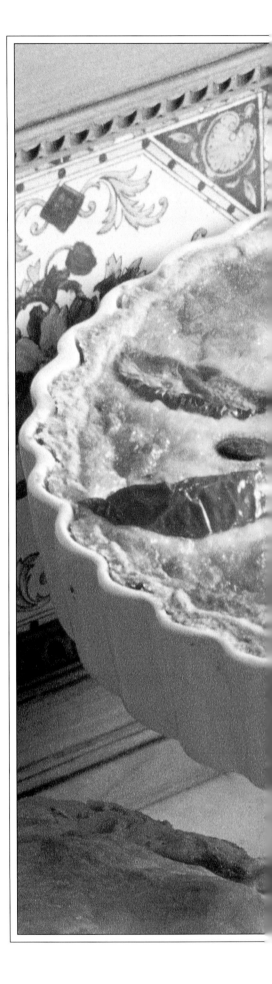

PIES

"To keep in health this rule is wise,
Eat only when you need and relish food,
Chew thoroughly that it may do you good.
Food for repentance—mince pie eaten late at night,
Have it well cooked, unspiced, and undisguised.
He who eats till he is sick must fast till he is —

ONE of the

PISSALADIÈRE

PASTRY:

6 oz (185 g) all-purpose (plain) flour
pinch of salt
3 oz (90 g) butter
approx. 2 tablespoons water

TOPPING:

2 tablespoons olive oil
2 medium white onions, thinly sliced
freshly ground pepper
3 tablespoons freshly grated parmesan cheese
5 large tomatoes, peeled and chopped
1 tablespoon tomato paste (purée) or tomato granules
8 anchovy filets
8 black olives, pitted (stoned) and halved

Sift flour and salt into a bowl and rub in butter. Add enough water to make a firm dough; knead lightly. Roll on a lightly-floured board and lay on a greased pizza tray. Pinch edges to decorate and prick base all over with a fork. Chill for 1 hour.

Preheat oven to 350°F (180°C, Gas Mark 4). Bake for 15 minutes, then take out of oven but leave the oven on.

Topping: Heat olive oil in a frying pan, and sauté onions for about 10 minutes or until tender. Remove from pan, cool slightly, then arrange on pastry. Sprinkle with pepper and grated parmesan cheese.

Put the chopped tomatoes and tomato paste in frying pan; cook for about 10 minutes or until moisture evaporates. Spoon tomato over cheese and sprinkle with a little more pepper. Arrange anchovies in a lattice design on top of tomatoes and put half an olive in each diamond.

Bake in oven for 10 minutes. Serve hot, with a green salad.

PIZZA SICILIANO

SERVES 4–6

PIZZA BASE:

3 oz (90 g) all-purpose (plain) flour

3 oz (90 g) self-rising (raising) flour

1/2 teaspoon dry (powdered) mustard

salt and cayenne

2 oz (60 g) butter or margarine

1 egg

3 tablespoons milk

1 tablespoon oil

TOPPING:

1 tablespoon oil

8 oz (250 g) lean ground (minced) steak or ham

1 white onion, chopped

1/2 clove garlic, crushed

3 medium tomatoes, peeled and chopped

4 oz (125 g) tasty cheese, grated

2 teaspoons anchovy extract (essence), optional

1 tablespoon chopped parsley

Preheat oven to 375°F (190°C, Gas Mark 5).

Pizza base: Sift together flours, mustard, salt, and cayenne. Rub in butter. Beat together egg and milk, and stir in dry ingredients. Mix to a firm dough. Knead lightly only until dough is smooth. Roll out to 1/8 inch (3 mm) thick and lay on a greased pizza tray. Brush liberally with oil.

Topping: Heat oil in a large pan, add steak, onion, and garlic. Sauté until meat browns and onion is tender. Spoon mixture into a bowl and cool.

Add remaining ingredients to mixture, bind well, and spread onto pizza base. Bake in oven for about 30 minutes. Cut into wedges, and serve hot.

POTATO-TOPPED FISH PIE

SERVES 4

8 oz (250 g) white fish filets
2 cups (16 fl oz, 500 ml) milk
6 scallops
1 1/2 oz (45 g) butter
1 heaped tablespoon all-purpose (plain) flour
6 oz (185 g) mushrooms, sliced
6 oz (185 g) shelled cooked shrimp (prawns), chopped
6 oysters, chopped
salt and pepper

TOPPING:

1 lb (500 g) potatoes, cooked and still hot
2 tablespoons finely chopped parsley
salt and pepper
little melted butter

Preheat oven to 425°F (220°C, Gas Mark 7).

Cut the fish into chunks, and poach in milk until tender enough to flake. Add scallops for last 3 or 4 minutes while fish is cooking. Drain, and reserve liquid; put fish in a bowl.

Melt 1 oz (30 g) of butter in a saucepan, blend in flour and cook for 3 minutes. Gradually whisk in poaching liquid, stirring constantly until mixture thickens.

Melt remaining butter and sauté mushrooms until just tender. Fold into fish mixture, add shrimps, oysters, salt, and pepper.

Butter a pie dish and spoon in a layer of fish and mushroom mixture. Cover with a layer of sauce, remainder of fish mixture, then remaining sauce.

Mash hot potatoes, stir in parsley, salt, and pepper. Spread evenly over pie mixture. Pour melted butter over, and roughen surface. Bake for 15 to 20 minutes.

SAVORY PUMPKIN PIE

SERVES 6–8

PASTRY:

4 oz (125g) butter or margarine, softened
2 tablespoons hot water
8 oz (250g) wholemeal self-raising flour
pinch of salt
3 tablespoon crushed nuts

FILLING:

1 1/2 cups cooked dry pumpkin
2 eggs, separated
2/3 cup (5 fl oz, 150 ml) sour cream
2/3 cup (5 fl oz, 150 ml) milk
1/2 teaspoon ground ginger
salt and pepper
3 oz (90 g) tasty cheese, grated
6 spring onions, finely chopped
2 teaspoons finely grated lemon peel
2 teaspoons Worcestershire sauce
1/2 teaspoon dried mustard
1 tablespoon finely chopped parsley

Preheat the oven to 325°F (160°C, Gas Mark 3). Place the butter in a bowl, pour on the hot water, and mash well with a fork. Add the flour and salt, add the nuts and work together until it is a soft dough. Allow to firm up in the refrigerator if necessary. Roll out and line (or press into) a 9 inch (23 cm) pie dish. Prick the base of the pastry well with a fork and bake "blind" for 10 to 15 minutes. Remove the "blind" filling and allow to cool.

Preheat the oven to 425°F (220°C, Gas Mark 7).

Filling: Mash the pumpkin, and beat in the egg yolks, cream, milk, ginger, salt, and pepper. Stir in the cheese, chopped spring onions, lemon peel, Worcestershire sauce, dried mustard and parsley. Beat the egg whites and fold into the mixture. Pour into the cold pastry shell and bake in the preheated oven for 15 minutes, then reduce the temperature to 325°F (160°C, Gas Mark 3) and continue baking for a further 35 minutes. Serve warm, with a crisp green salad.

WHOLEWHEAT PIZZA PIE

SERVES 6

DOUGH:

1/2 oz (15 g) fresh yeast or 1/4 oz (7 g) dried yeast
2 teaspoons molasses or honey
1 cup (8 fl oz, 250 ml) lukewarm water
2 cups (8 oz, 240 g) plain flour
2 cups (8 oz, 240 g) wholemeal flour
pinch of salt
1 tablespoon soft margarine

TOPPING:

1 can/ 1 lb 14 oz (825 g) tomatoes
2 white onions, finely chopped
1/2 clove garlic, crushed
1 teaspoon raw sugar
1/2 teaspoon dried basil or 1 teaspoon fresh chopped basil
1/2 teaspoon oregano or 1 teaspoon fresh chopped oregano
salt and pepper
1/2 cup (4 oz, 120 g) cooked soya beans
1 tablespoon oil, for brushing
6 oz (185 g) tasty cheese, grated
4 oz (125 g) mushrooms, sliced
6 green or black olives, pitted and slivered
4 oz (125 g) mozzarella cheese, sliced

In a medium-sized bowl, blend together the yeast and molasses or honey. Stir in warm water, and leave in a warm place until the mixture froths.

In a large bowl, combine the flours and salt. Rub in the margarine. Make a well in middle, and pour in yeast liquid, stirring until mixed. Tip dough onto a lightly floured board and knead for 5 minutes. Return it to the bowl, cover with a kitchen (tea) towel, and leave it to rise until it doubles in size. Preheat the oven to 400°F (200°C , Gas Mark 6).

While dough is rising, prepare filling. Chop tomatoes and spoon them into a saucepan with liquid from the can. Add onions, garlic, sugar, herbs, salt, and pepper, and simmer gently until mixture thickens. Stir in soya beans.

Punch dough down with fist, and roll it to fit a lightly-greased pizza tray. Prick surface in several places, then brush with oil. Sprinkle pizza dough with grated cheese, then spoon tomato mixture over it, spreading evenly. Arrange mushroom slices and slivered olives, then arrange sliced mozzarella cheese in a circle on top. Bake for about 30 minutes.

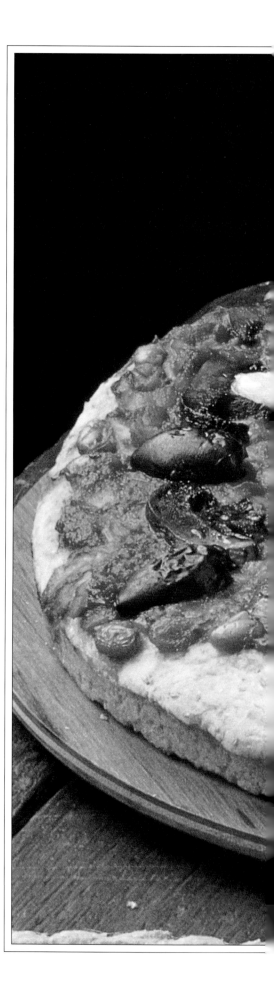

ALMOND & POPPY SEED PIE

FILLING:

1 apple

3/4 cup (3 oz, 90 g) ground almonds

3/4 cup (3 oz, 90 g) ground poppy seeds

1/2 cup (4 fl oz, 125 ml) milk

1/4 cup (2 fl oz, 60 ml) cream

1/4 cup (1 1/2 oz, 45 g) currants

1/4 cup (2 oz, 60 g) sugar

1 tablespoon honey

1 oz (30 g) butter

1 teaspoon ground cinnamon

grated rind of 1/2 lemon

grated rind of 1/2 orange

PASTRY:

6 oz (185 g) filo pastry

4 oz (125 g) butter, melted

confectioners' (icing) sugar, for sprinkling

Filling: Peel and grate apple into a bowl. Add remaining filling ingredients and place bowl over a pan of simmering water. Cook, stirring continuously, until very thick (about 20 minutes). Remove from heat and cool.

Preheat oven to 350°F (180°C, Gas Mark 4). Brush a sheet of filo pastry with melted butter. Lay butter side down in a 9 inch (23 cm) pie plate. Brush with melted butter and lay another sheet of filo pastry over. Brush with melted butter and repeat with three more layers of pastry. Spoon filling onto pastry and smooth surface. Top filling with about five more sheets of pastry, brushing each one with melted butter. Trim off edges with a sharp knife.

Bake in oven for 30 to 40 minutes or until crisp and golden. Sprinkle with confectioners' sugar, and slice with a serrated knife. Serve warm or at room temperature.

APPLE AMBER

RICH SHORTCRUST PASTRY:

1 1/2 cups (6 oz, 185 g) all-purpose (plain) flour
3 oz (90 g) unsalted butter, chilled
3/4 tablespoon superfine (caster) sugar
pinch of salt, optional
1 egg yolk
1 1/2 teaspoons lemon juice
1–1 1/2 tablespoons cold water

FILLING:

1 lb (500 g) green cooking apples
3 tablespoons brown sugar
1 lemon
1 tablespoon water
1 1/2 oz (45 g) butter
2 eggs, separated
2 tablespoons superfine (caster) sugar for meringue
extra superfine (caster) sugar, for sprinkling

Rich shortcrust pastry: Sift flour into a cold mixing bowl. Cut butter into flour with a palette knife, then rub into flour with fingertips until mixture resembles breadcrumbs, stir in sugar, and salt with the knife. Mix egg yolk and lemon juice together, sprinkle over mixture, then mix together with the knife. Gradually mix in sufficient cold water until mixture forms lumps which leave sides of bowl cleanly. Knead dough together lightly with a clean, cool hand. You can use an electric mixer or food processor.

Turn dough onto a lightly-floured surface and knead until smooth underneath. Turn over and pat into a round cake shape 1/2–1 inch (1–2.5 cm) thick. Wrap in waxed (greaseproof) paper and chill for 30 minutes before use.

Preheat oven to 350°F (180°C, Gas Mark 4).

Filling: Peel, core, and slice apples. Place apples, sugar, strips of lemon rind, and water in a saucepan; cover, and cook gently until apple is very soft. Remove lemon rind and purée apple in a food processor. Cut butter into small pieces and add with egg yolks and lemon juice to the purée. Blend well.

Roll out pastry and line a deep 9 inch (23 cm) pie dish. Crimp edges, and brush with a little lightly-beaten egg white. Pour in apple mixture. Bake for 30 minutes or until pastry is crisp and golden.

Meringue topping: whisk egg whites until stiff, then with a large metal spoon gently fold in sugar. When pastry is cooked and golden, remove from oven, and increase temperature to 375°F (190°C, Gas Mark 5). Pile meringue on top of apple, taking meringue right to edge of pastry. Sprinkle with a little extra sugar. Bake for 15 minutes or until meringue is golden. Serve warm or cold.

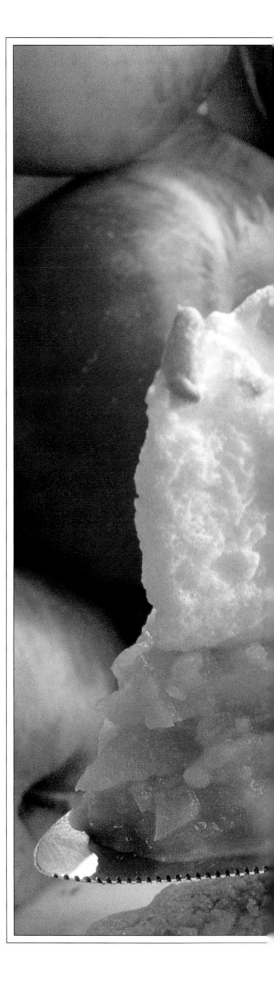

BAKEWELL TART

SWEET SHORTCRUST PASTRY:

1 1/2 cups (6 oz, 185 g) all-purpose (plain) flour
pinch of salt, optional
1 1/2 oz (45 g) chilled butter or firm margarine
1 1/2 oz (45 g) shortening (lard)
3/4 tablespoon superfine (caster) sugar
approx 3 tablespoons cold water

FILLING:

3 oz (90 g) soft butter or margarine
1/3 cup (3 oz, 90 g) superfine (caster) sugar
2 large eggs
1/2 cup (2 oz, 60 g) ground almonds
1/2 cup (2 oz, 60 g) self-rising (raising) flour, sifted
drops of almond extract (essence)
3 tablespoons raspberry jelly (jam)
6 split almonds, for decoration
confectioners' (icing) sugar, for sprinkling

Sweet shortcrust pastry: Sift flour and salt into cold mixing bowl. Cut in butter and shortening with a palette knife, coating with flour. Rub fat into flour with cool fingertips, lifting up and rubbing from a height to lighten and aerate.

When mixture resembles breadcrumbs, shake bowl gently and any lumps will rise to surface. Squeeze and if dry, fat is rubbed in sufficiently, but if they feel greasy, continue rubbing in. Mix in sugar.

Sprinkle cold water over gradually and mix in with a palette knife until mixture begins to form lumps which leave side of bowl cleanly. Knead dough together lightly with a clean, cool hand.

You can use an electric mixer or a food processor. Chill well.

Roll pastry out thinly in a round, and line a deep-sided 8 inch (20 cm) flan dish. Reserve pastry trimmings; and prick base of the pastry case.

Filling: Place all ingredients except jelly and split almonds in a mixing bowl and beat well with an electric mixer or in a food processor until well mixed (about 1–2 minutes).

Preheat oven to 350°F (180°C, Gas Mark 4). Spread jelly over base of pastry, spread with filling. Roll pastry trimmings into a long strip and cut strips 3/4 inch (1 cm) wide; lay on tart in a lattice pattern, and trim neatly. Decorate top of tart with split almonds.

Bake in middle of oven for 45 to 50 minutes, until cooked. Cool on a wire rack. Serve warm, sprinkled with confectioners' sugar, accompanied by custard or cream.

BANANA CHIFFON PIE

SERVES 6–8

RICH SHORTCRUST PASTRY:

1 1/2 cups (6 oz, 185 g) all-purpose (plain) flour
3 oz (90 g) unsalted butter, chilled
3/4 tablespoon superfine (caster) sugar
pinch of salt, optional
1 egg yolk
1 1/2 teaspoons lemon juice
1–1 1/2 tablespoons cold water

FILLING:

1 1/2 teaspoons jello (gelatin)
2 tablespoons hot water
3/4 cup mashed banana (approx 2 large bananas)
grated rind and juice of 1 lemon
2 eggs, separated
1/2 cup (4 oz, 125 g) superfine (caster) sugar

Rich shortcrust pastry: Sift flour into a cold mixing bowl. Cut butter into flour with a palette knife, then rub into flour with fingertips until mixture resembles breadcrumbs, stir in sugar, and salt with the knife. Mix egg yolk and lemon juice together, sprinkle over mixture, then mix together with the knife. Gradually mix in sufficient cold water until mixture forms lumps which leave sides of bowl cleanly. Knead dough together lightly with a clean, cool hand. You can use an electric mixer or food processor.

Turn dough onto a lightly-floured surface and knead until smooth underneath. Turn over and pat into a round cake shape 1/2–1 inch (1–2.5 cm) thick. Wrap in waxed (greaseproof) paper and chill for 30 minutes before use.

Preheat oven to 425°F (220°C, Gas Mark 7). Roll out pastry on a lightly floured surface and line a 9 inch (23 cm) pie plate. Bake "blind" for 10 minutes. Remove baking beans and paper, reduce oven temperature to 375°F (190°C, Gas Mark 5) and bake for a further 10 minutes. Cool on a wire rack.

Filling: Sprinkle jello over 2 tablespoons of hot water to dissolve. In blender or food processor blend bananas until mashed — but not puréed. Place 3/4 cup of the mashed bananas in a heavy-based saucepan. Add lemon rind and lemon juice. Stir in egg yolks and 3 tablespoons of sugar and cook, stirring constantly, over a moderate heat until mixture thickens. Remove from heat and add dissolved jello. Cool mixture until just beginning to set.

Whisk egg whites until stiff. Gradually add remaining sugar and beat until the texture of smooth meringue. Fold into banana mixture, and spoon into pie case. Chill until ready to serve.

CHERRY PIE

SERVES 6-8

PASTRY:

2 cups (8 oz, 250 g) self-rising (raising) flour
4 oz (125 g) shortening (lard)
5 tablespoons water
pinch of salt

FILLING:

20 oz (625 g) pitted (stoned), stewed, drained cherries
1 cup (8 fl oz, 250 ml) cherry juice
$^1/_2$ cup (4 oz, 125 g) sugar
$^1/_2$ teaspoon salt
2 drops almond extract (essence)
1 tablespoon fine tapioca
1 tablespoon melted butter
egg white, for glazing
superfine (caster) sugar, for glazing

Pastry: Sift flour into a bowl and cut in shortening; rub in until mixture resembles fine breadcrumbs. Add water, and mix in with a knife until a rough dough forms. Refrigerate dough to 30 minutes.

Filling: Combine all ingredients for the filling, and stand for 15 minutes.

Preheat oven to 375°F (190°C, Gas Mark 5). Line a deep 8 inch (20 cm) pie dish with two-thirds of the pastry. Fill with cherry mixture. Roll out remaining pastry and use to cover pie. Pinch edges, and make four slits on top of pastry. Glaze pastry with egg white, and sprinkle sugar over top. Bake for 35 minutes.

FRENCH APPLE FLANS

PÂTE SUCRÉE:

6 oz (175 g) all purpose (plain) flour
pinch of salt
3 oz (90 g) superfine (caster) sugar
3 oz (90 g) butter, softened
3 egg yolks

FILLING:

1 lb (900 g) cooking apples, peeled, cored and sliced
4 tablespoons water
10 oz (300 g) apricot jam, sieved
superfine (caster) sugar to taste
3 dessert apples
juice of ¹/₂ lemon
1 oz (30 g) butter, melted
1 tablespoon water

Pastry: sift the flour and salt onto a flat surface, make a well in the middle and add the sugar, butter and egg yolks. Using the fingertips, pinch and work these ingredients together then gradually work in the flour to give a smooth pliable dough. Wrap in plastic (cling) wrap or foil and chill for an hour.

Roll out the pastry and use to line eight individual flan pans or Yorkshire pudding pans about 3¹/₂–4 inches (9–10 cm) in diameter. Bake blind in a moderately hot oven (375°F, 190°C, Gas Mark 5) for 5–10 minutes, remove the paper and beans and return to the oven for a couple of minutes to dry out. Cool on a wire rack.

Place the apples and water in a saucepan and cook for about 20 minutes to make a smooth purée. Add a third of the apricot jam and the sugar to taste, and simmer very gently until the purée is very thick. Allow to cool.

Roll the pastry out thinly and use to line eight induvidual fluted flan pans of about 4–4¹/₂ inches (12–14 cm) in diameter.

Spoon cold apple purée into the lined pans, levelling the top. Peel, core and slice dessert apples. Place in a bowl with the lemon juice (to prevent browning); arrange in overlapping slices to cover the apple purée. Brush lightly with melted butter.

Cook in a moderately hot oven (400°F, 200°C, Gas Mark 6) for about 35–40 minutes or until the apples are lightly browned and the pastry cooked through.

Place the remaining sieved apricot jam in a saucepan with the water and heat until the glaze thickens sufficiently to cover the back of the spoon.

Brush the warm glaze over the apple slices and the top edges of the pastry flans as soon as they come out of the oven. Leave to cool in the pans and then remove carefully to serve.

FRESH MINT PIE

SERVES 6–8

CRUMB CRUST:

8 oz (225 g) packet wholewheat (wholemeal) or plain sweet biscuits
4 oz (125 g) butter

FILLING:

2 oz (60 g) semi-sweet (dark) chocolate
3 oz (90 g) unsalted butter
1 1/2 cup (8 oz, 250 g) confectioners' (icing) sugar
2 large eggs
2 1/2 cups (20 fl oz, 600 ml) light (single) cream
drops of peppermint extract (essence)
chopped walnuts, to decorate

Crumb crust: Break biscuits in half into a blender or food processor, about a third at a time, then mix at maximum speed for 20 seconds or until biscuits are crushed. Pour biscuit crumbs into a bowl.

Melt butter in a saucepan over a low heat; add to biscuit crumbs and mix thoroughly. Cool slightly, then press into a 9 inch (23 cm) pie plate. Refrigerate until firm (about 1 hour). Bake in a preheated oven at 375°F (190°C, Gas Mark 5) for 10 minutes. Cool.

Melt chocolate on a plate over a pan of simmering water. Cool.

Beat butter and sugar together until light and creamy. Beat cooled chocolate into butter mixture with eggs until mixture is light and fluffy.

Whip cream until it holds its shape; fold half into chocolate mixture. Stir in a couple of drops of peppermint to taste, and spoon mixture into pie case. Chill until filling is firm.

Decorate with remaining cream and chopped walnuts.

FRUIT MINCE PIES

MAKES 12 PIES

SHORTCRUST PASTRY:

1/2 cup (4 oz, 125 g) unsalted butter or margarine, chilled
2 cups (8 oz, 250 g) all-purpose (plain) flour
1/2 cup (2 oz, 60 g) pure confectioners' (icing) sugar
2 egg yolks or 1 egg
1 teaspoon water (only if necessary)

FILLING:

1 cup (5 oz, 155 g) fruit mincemeat
beaten egg, for glazing
superfine (caster) sugar, for sprinkling

Pastry: Cut butter into cubes. Sift flour and sugar together. Add butter to flour mixture to butter and mix at top speed in a mixer or rub in the butter with tips of the fingers until mixture resembles fine breadcrumbs.

Add egg and mix until dough comes together; add water only if dough will not bind. Knead dough very lightly until smooth, then wrap in waxed (greaseproof) paper and chill for 30 minutes or until firm.

Preheat oven to 375°F, (190°C, Gas Mark 5). Assemble twelve small (individual-serving), deep pie tins, and line six of them at a time. Roll out half the pastry into a rectangle. Gently lift it and lay it over six pie tins. Lightly press the pastry into the tins, and roll the rolling pin over to cut the edges; gather pastry off-cuts into a ball and set aside for the pie tops. Roll out the second half of the pastry and line the other six tins. (Alternatively, cut the pastry into rounds using a cutter, and line the pie tins.)

Spoon about 2 teaspoons of mincemeat into each pie.

Roll out the off-cuts and, using a tiny star cutter, cut twelve pastry stars for each pie top. Lay a top over each pie and brush with beaten egg. Sprinkle with sugar and place the pie tins on a baking sheet (oven tray).

Bake in the preheated oven for 25 minutes or until pale golden brown. Serve warm or cold.

GÂTEAU DE PITHIVIERS FEUILLETÉ

SERVES 6–8

PUFF PASTRY:

12 oz (375 g) unsalted butter
3 cups (12 oz, 375 g) all-purpose (plain) flour
pinch of salt, optional
1 teaspoon lemon juice
cold water, to mix

FILLING:

4 oz (125 g) butter
¹/₂ cup (4 oz, 125 g) superfine (caster) sugar
1 egg
1¹/₄ cups (4 oz, 125 g) ground almonds
2 teaspoons all-purpose (plain) flour
1 teaspoon vanilla extract (essence)
beaten egg, for glazing
extra superfine (caster) sugar, for glazing

Puff pastry: Make and cool pastry according to instructions for *Economical Steak and Kidney Pie* (page 12).

Filling: Cream butter and sugar until pale and creamy. Beat in egg. Stir in ground almonds, flour, and vanilla.

Preheat oven to 425°F (220°C, Gas Mark 7). Roll out half pastry on a lightly-floured surface, into a round 11 inch (28 cm) across. Using a saucepan lid, cut a circle 10 inches (25 cm) across, slightly angling knife away from the lid. Roll out remaining pastry slightly thicker and cut into a 10 inch (25 cm) round. Place thinnest circle on a baking tray, and mound filling in the middle, leaving a 1 inch (2.5 cm) border. Brush edge with water and place the second pastry round over filling. Press edges together firmly. Scallop edges and brush with beaten egg glaze. Working from middle, score top in curves like flower petals. Chill for 15 minutes.

Bake for 30 to 35 minutes or until firm and puffed. Sprinkle top with superfine sugar and put pie under a hot broiler (grill) until sugar has caramelized and surface is shiny. Cool on a wire rack.

JAFFA CHIFFON PIE

SERVES 6-8

RICH SHORTCRUST PASTRY:

1 1/2 cups (6 oz, 185 g) all-purpose (plain) flour

3 oz (90 g) unsalted butter, chilled

3/4 tablespoon superfine (caster) sugar

pinch of salt, optional

1 egg yolk

1 1/2 teaspoons lemon juice

1–1 1/2 tablespoons cold water

CRUMB CRUST:

8 oz (225 g) packet plain sweet chocolate biscuits

4 oz (125 g) butter

FILLING:

1 teaspoon jello (gelatin)

1 tablespoon hot water

3 eggs, separated

1/3 cup (3 oz, 90 g) superfine (caster) sugar

1 tablespoon orange juice

3 oz (90 g) semi-sweet (dark) chocolate

grated rind of 1 orange

2 tablespoons whipped cream

Rich shortcrust pastry: Sift flour into a cold mixing bowl. Cut butter into flour with a palette knife, then rub into flour with fingertips until mixture resembles breadcrumbs, stir in sugar, and salt with the knife. Mix egg yolk and lemon juice together, sprinkle over mixture, then mix together with the knife. Gradually mix in sufficient cold water until mixture forms lumps which leave sides of bowl cleanly. Knead dough together lightly with a clean, cool hand. Turn dough onto a lightly-floured surface and knead until smooth underneath. Turn over and pat into a round cake shape 1/2–1 inch (1–2.5 cm) thick. Wrap in waxed (greaseproof) paper and chill for 30 minutes before use. Preheat oven to 375°F (190°C, Gas Mark 5). Roll out pastry on a lightly-floured surface and use it to line a 9 inch (23 cm) pie plate. Bake "blind" for 10 minutes. Remove baking beans and paper, bake for a further 10 minutes or until golden and crisp. Cool.

Crumb crust: Bake for 10 minutes. Cool.

Filling: Dissolve jello in hot water. Whisk egg yolks, half sugar and orange juice in a bowl over simmering water; beat until thick and pale, remove from heat. Melt chocolate on a plate over simmering water; stir into egg yolk mixture with orange rind and dissolved jello. Whisk mixture until thick and light and just about to set. Whisk egg whites with remaining sugar, and fold through chocolate and orange mixture with whipped cream. Spoon into pie case, and chill until ready to serve.

KIWI FRUIT TART

SERVES 8–12

SHORTCRUST PASTRY:

1/2 cup (4 oz, 125 g) unsalted butter or margarine, chilled
2 cups (8 oz, 250 g) all-purpose (plain) flour
1/2 cup (2 oz, 60 g) pure confectioners' (icing) sugar
2 egg yolks or 1 egg
1 teaspoon water (only if necessary)

FILLING:

2 lb (1 kg) kiwifruit, approx 12 large or 18 small
1/4 cup ground almonds
4 tablespoons vanilla sugar
2 x 2 oz (60 g) eggs
5 tablespoons cream or orange soy drink
1 tablespoon orange flower water

Pastry: Cut butter into cubes. Sift flour and sugar together. Add butter to flour mixture to butter and mix at top speed in a mixer or rub in the butter with tips of the fingers until mixture resembles fine breadcrumbs.

Add egg and mix until dough comes together; add water only if dough will not bind. Knead dough very lightly until smooth, then wrap in waxed (greaseproof) paper and chill for 30 minutes or until firm.

Roll pastry out thinly to a round and line a 12 inch (30 cm) flan tin. Trim and neaten edge, prick base and chill until filling is ready.

Filling: Peel kiwifruit with a vegetable peeler and cut into 1/4 inch (5 mm) slices. Beat all the remaining ingredients together.

To finish tart: Arrange kiwifruit, overlapping slices in circles in the pastry case, starting at edge, working into middle. Pour egg mixture over and brush over any fruit that is not coated.

Bake at 425°F (220°C, Gas Mark 7) for 25 to 30 minutes or until filling is firm. Serve warm or cold sifted with confectioners' (icing) sugar if desired.

MINCE TART

SERVES 8

SWEET SHORTCRUST PASTRY:

6 oz (185 g) flour
pinch of salt, optional
1 1/2 oz (45 g) chilled butter or firm margarine
1 1/2 oz (45 g) shortening (lard)
3/4 tablespoon superfine (caster) sugar
approx. 3 tablespoons cold water

FILLING:

2 cups (16 oz, 500 g) fruit mincemeat
1 cup (8 oz, 250 g) stewed apple
beaten egg and superfine (caster) sugar, for glazing
confectioners' (icing) sugar, for decoration

Sweet shortcrust pastry: Sift flour and salt into cold mixing bowl. Cut in butter and shortening with a palette knife, coating with flour. Rub fat into flour with cool fingertips, lifting up and rubbing from a height to lighten and aerate.

When mixture resembles breadcrumbs, shake bowl gently and any lumps will rise to surface. Squeeze and if dry, fat is rubbed in sufficiently, but if they feel greasy, continue rubbing in. Mix in sugar.

Sprinkle cold water over gradually and mix in with a palette knife until mixture begins to form lumps which leave side of bowl cleanly. Knead dough together lightly with a clean, cool hand.

You can use an electric mixer or a food processor. Chill well.

Roll three-quarters of pastry into a thin round, and line a 9 or 10 inch (23 or 25 cm) flan dish, trim and neaten edge, prick base and chill for 30 minutes.

Mix fruit mincemeat with stewed apple.

Bake pastry case "blind", near top of a preheated oven at 425°F (220°C, Gas Mark 7) for 10 minutes. Remove "blind" filling, and spread fruit-mince on pastry. Roll out remaining pastry in a thin rectangle then cut into strips 3/8 inch (1 cm) wide; lay these on tart in a lattice pattern and trim edges. Glaze pastry with beaten egg and sprinkle with sugar. Reduce oven to 350°F (180°C, Gas Mark 4), bake near the top for 25 minutes or until cooked. Serve warm or cold sifted generously with sugar, accompanied by whipped cream or ice cream.

ORANGE ALMOND PIE

SERVES 6–8

RICH SHORTCRUST PASTRY:

1 1/2 cups (6 oz, 185 g) all-purpose (plain) flour

3 oz (90 g) unsalted butter, chilled

3/4 tablespoon superfine (caster) sugar

pinch of salt, optional

1 egg yolk

1 1/2 teaspoons lemon juice

1–1 1/2 tablespoons cold water

FILLING:

4 oz (125 g) unsalted butter

1/3 cup confectioners' (icing) sugar

2 large eggs

1 cup (4 oz, 125 g) blanched almonds, ground

2 tablespoons flour

5 large navel oranges

1 tablespoon Cointreau or Grand Marnier

2 tablespoons confectioners' (icing) sugar

1/2 cup (4 oz, 125 g) sieved orange marmalade

1 tablespoon toasted sliced almonds for decoration (optional)

Rich shortcrust pastry: Make and chill the pastry according to instructions for *Apple Amber* (page 32).

Preheat the oven to 425°F (220°C, Gas Mark 7). Roll the pastry out thinly and line a 9 inch (23 cm) pie dish. Prick the base of the pie crust. Bake blind near the top of the oven for 10 minutes. Remove the blind filling and bake for another 10 minutes, until golden, then allow to cool on a wire rack.

Filling: Cream butter and sugar together. Add eggs one at a time and beat well. Stir in ground almonds and flour until evenly mixed. Peel oranges, cut the segments away from the membrane. Sprinkle the liqueur and sugar over the segments; cover and soak for 30 minutes. Reduce the oven to 350°F (180°C, Gas Mark 4). Spread the almond mixture into the pie crust and bake in the middle of the oven for 20 to 25 minutes or until golden and a skewer comes out fairly dry. Cool on a wire rack.

Transfer the orange segments to a plate with a slotted spoon and pat them dry with kitchen paper towels; reserve the liquid. Place the sieved marmalade and 2 tablespoons of reserved orange liquid into a saucepan; bring to a boil, stirring continuously. Simmer for 1 minute, then cool for 1 minute. Brush the marmalade glaze over the top of the pie, arrange the orange segments in circles on it, then brush with more glaze. Decorate the pie with toasted sliced almonds, if desired.

PEAR & HAZELNUT PIE

SERVES 4-6

PASTRY:

2 cups (8 oz, 250 g) all-purpose (plain) flour
pinch of salt
1/2 cup (2 oz, 60 g) ground filberts (hazelnuts)
2 teaspoons ground cinnamon
5 oz (155 g) butter
1/2 cup (4 oz, 125 g) superfine (caster) sugar
2–3 drops vanilla extract (essence)
1 egg
1 tablespoon water

FILLING:

3–4 ripe dessert pears
approx 1 tablespoon superfine (caster) sugar
whipped cream, for serving

Pastry: Sift flour and salt onto a work surface. Make a large well in the middle. Sprinkle ground filberts and cinnamon into the middle and make another well using palm of your hand. Place butter in middle of well and make a depression in the slab. Sprinkle over sugar and break egg on top; add vanilla. Pinch butter, sugar, and egg together using tips of your fingers, until combined. Draw filberts and flour into the middle with a spatula. Add tablespoon of water to dough if needed. Gather dough together and wrap in a sheet of waxed (greaseproof) paper. Chill for 15 minutes.

Preheat oven to 375°F (190°C, Gas Mark 5).

Filling: Peel and quarter pears, remove core.

Roll out two-thirds of pastry on a lightly-floured surface and use to line a shallow 8 inch (20 cm) pie plate. Arrange pear quarters over base and sprinkle with some sugar. Roll remaining pastry into a round, large enough to cover pie; and cut a 2 1/2 inch (6 cm) circle out of the middle. Lay pastry over pears, and trim edges. Press edges together with the back of a fork or knife. Bake for 35 minutes or until evenly golden brown. Sprinkle with a little more sugar, and return to oven for a few minutes. Cook on a rack. Serve warm, with lightly-whipped cream.

PECAN PIE

SERVES 6

RICH SHORTCRUST PASTRY:

1 1/2 cups (6 oz, 185 g) all-purpose (plain) flour
3 oz (90 g) unsalted butter, chilled
3/4 tablespoon superfine (caster) sugar
pinch of salt, optional
1 egg yolk
1 1/2 teaspoons lemon juice
1–1 1/2 tablespoons cold water

FILLING:

3 oz (90 g) butter
1 cup (8 fl oz, 250 ml) light corn syrup (golden syrup)
1/2 teaspoon salt
1 cup (7 oz, 220 g) sugar
4 eggs
2 cups (8 oz, 250 g) pecan halves
1 teaspoon vanilla extract (essence)

Rich shortcrust pastry: Sift flour into a cold mixing bowl. Cut butter into flour with a palette knife, then rub into flour with fingertips until mixture resembles breadcrumbs, stir in sugar, and salt with the knife. Mix egg yolk and lemon juice together, sprinkle over mixture, then mix together with the knife. Gradually mix in sufficient cold water until mixture forms lumps which leave sides of bowl cleanly. Knead dough together lightly with a clean, cool hand. You can use an electric mixer or food processor.

Turn dough onto a lightly-floured surface and knead until smooth underneath. Turn over and pat into a round cake shape 1/2–1 inch (1–2.5 cm) thick. Wrap in waxed (greaseproof) paper and chill for 30 minutes before use.

Roll out pastry on a lightly-floured surface and use to line a 9 inch (23 cm) pie plate. Chill.

Preheat oven to 375°F (190°C, Gas Mark 5).

Filling: Melt butter and stir in corn syrup, salt, sugar, and eggs. Mix well to combine. Add nuts and vanilla. Pour filling into pie case, laying pecan nuts face upwards. Bake for 35 to 40 minutes or until filling is cooked and pastry golden brown. Serve warm or cold, with pouring cream.

SHORTBREAD PIE

SERVES 6

1 1/2 cups (6 oz, 185 g) all-purpose (plain) flour
pinch of salt
7 oz (220 g) butter
1/3 cup (2 oz, 60 g) confectioners' (icing) sugar
2 egg yolks
drops of vanilla extract (essence)
1 1/3 cups (5 oz, 170 g) ground almonds
3/4 cup (8 oz, 250 g) raspberry or blackberry jelly (jam), slightly warmed
1/4 cup (1 oz, 30 g) flaked almonds
confectioners' (icing) sugar, for sprinkling

Sift flour and salt onto a board. Make a well in the middle and add butter, sugar, egg yolks, and vanilla. Sprinkle ground almonds onto flour. Work ingredients in the middle with fingertips until thoroughly blended. Using a metal spatula, quickly draw in flour and ground almonds. Knead dough lightly, then chill for at least 1 hour.

Preheat oven to 325°F (160°C, Gas Mark 3).

Grate dough on a coarse grater into a greased 8 inch (20 cm) pie dish, using about two-thirds of the quantity to cover base thickly with dough. Spread with slightly warmed jelly (jam), then grate remaining dough over jelly (jam). Press lightly into dish, and sprinkle with flaked almonds. Bake for 1 1/4 hours. Cool.

When cold, sprinkle top thickly with sugar. Serve straight from dish with whipped cream.

STRAWBERRY SYLLABUB TARTS

SERVES 4–6

PÂTE SUCRÉE:

4 oz (125 g) all purpose (plain) flour
pinch of salt
2 oz (60 g) superfine (caster) sugar
2 oz (60 g) butter, softened
2 egg yolks
few drops vanilla extract

SYLLABUB FILLING:

1 egg white
2 oz (60 g) superfine (caster) sugar
finely grated peel (rind) of $^1/_2$ lemon
a good pinch of finely grated orange peel (rind)
2 teaspoons lemon juice
4 tablespoons dry white wine
$^2/_3$ cup (5 fl oz / 150 ml) heavy (double) cream
about 6 oz (175 g) strawberries
3 tablespoons redcurrant jelly
1 tablespoon water

Pastry cases: sift the flour and salt into a pile on a flat surface and make a well in the middle. Add the sugar, butter, egg yolks and extract.

Work the sugar mixture together then gradually work in the flour to give a smooth pliable dough. Wrap in foil and chill for 20–30 minutes.

Roll out the pastry and use to line four individual flan pans 4–4$^1/_2$ inches (10–11 cm) in diameter or six deep fluted pans 3 inches (7$^1/_2$ cm) in diameter. Prick bases and bake blind in a moderately hot oven (375°F/190°C, Gas Mark 5) for about 15 minutes; remove, then return to the oven for about 5 minutes to dry out and turn a light golden brown. Cool.

Syllabub filling: whisk the egg white until very stiff then fold in the sugar followed by the fruit peels, lemon juice and wine. Whip the cream until stiff and fold through the syllabub mixture.

Fill the pastry cases with the Syllabub an hour before serving. If the strawberries are small they may be used whole or halved to place on top of the syllabub, if not, slice them and arrange attractively over the filling. Melt the redcurrant jelly with the water and boil for approximately 1 minute. Cool slightly, then carefully spoon or brush over the strawberries. Chill until ready to serve.

Published by Harbour Books
PO Box 48, Millers Point NSW 2000, Australia

First published in 1996
Reprinted 1997

© Copyright: Harbour Books 1996
© Copyright design: Harbour Books 1996

ISBN 1 86302 505 7

All rights reserved. Subject to the Copyright Act 1968, no part of this
publication may be reproduced, stored in a retrieval
system, or transmitted, in any form, or by any means, electronic,
mechanical, photocopying, recording or otherwise, without the prior
written permission of the publisher.